Oklahoma City

THUNDER

BY K.C. KELLEY

Published by The Child's World®
1980 Lookout Drive • Mankato, MN 56003-1705
800-599-READ • www.childsworld.com

Cover: © Joe Robbins.
Interior Photographs ©: AP Images: Morry Gash 13; 17; Randy Rasmussen 29. Dreamstime.com: Justin Brotton 13. Imagn/USA Today Sports: Isaiah J. Downing 6; Alonzo Adams 10, 21; Jayne Kamin-Oncea 25; Bill Streicher 26; Steve Dykes 26. Newscom: Karl Wright/Icon SMI 9; Jim Bryant/UPI 18; Icon Sports Media 22; Brian Rothmuller/Icon SMI 26; Hector Amezcua 26. Joe Robbins: 5.

ISBN 9781503824720
LCCN 2018964291

Printed in the United States of America
PA02416

ABOUT THE AUTHOR

K.C. Kelley is a huge sports fan who has written more than 150 books for kids. He has written about football, basketball, soccer, and even auto racing! He lives in Santa Barbara, California.

TABLE OF
CONTENTS

GO, THUNDER!

In 2005, **Hurricane** Katrina smashed into New Orleans. It was a terrible storm. The NBA's New Orleans Hornets lost their home court. The team played two seasons in Oklahoma City. Fans there loved seeing the NBA! In 2008, the Seattle SuperSonics got a new owner. He saw what had happened after Katrina, and he moved his team to Oklahoma City. The team was re-named the Thunder. Since then, fans have packed Thunder games. A bad storm had a good ending!

Russell Westbrook points the way for the Thunder. The superstar guard is one of the top players in the NBA.

Oklahoma City's Steven Adams can handle it even when an opponent tries to climb over him!

WHO ARE THE THUNDER?

The Oklahoma City Thunder are one of 30 NBA teams. The Thunder play in the Northwest Division of the Western Conference. The other Northwest Division teams are the Denver Nuggets, the Minnesota Timberwolves, the Portland Trail Blazers, and the Utah Jazz. The Thunder have tough battles with their Northwest Division rivals!

WHERE THEY CAME FROM

In 1967, the NBA added two new teams. One of them was the Seattle SuperSonics. The team often made the playoffs. Fans saw some great teams. In 2008, a new owner moved the team to Oklahoma City. As the Thunder, the team has had some of its best seasons. The Thunder has missed the playoffs only twice in Oklahoma City.

Ray Allen's uniform shows off the old nickname of the team that became the Thunder.

The Thunder's Jerami Grant leaps to make a shot over an Eastern Conference foe, the Chicago Bulls.

WHO THEY PLAY

The Thunder play 82 games each season. They play 41 games at home and 41 on the road. The Thunder play four games against each of the other Northwest Division teams. They play 36 games against other Western Conference teams. The Thunder also play each of the teams in the Eastern Conference twice. That's a lot of basketball! Each June, the winners of the Western and Eastern Conferences play each other in the NBA Finals.

The Thunder is the only major pro sports team in Oklahoma. Fans pack the Chesapeake Energy Arena for every game. People often wear white T-shirts. The whole arena looks like a snowstorm! Fans get help cheering from Rumble. This large, fuzzy bison is the team's **mascot**.

13

Rumble does dunks at halftime. Fans at the Thunder's arena (left) love to see a bison fly!

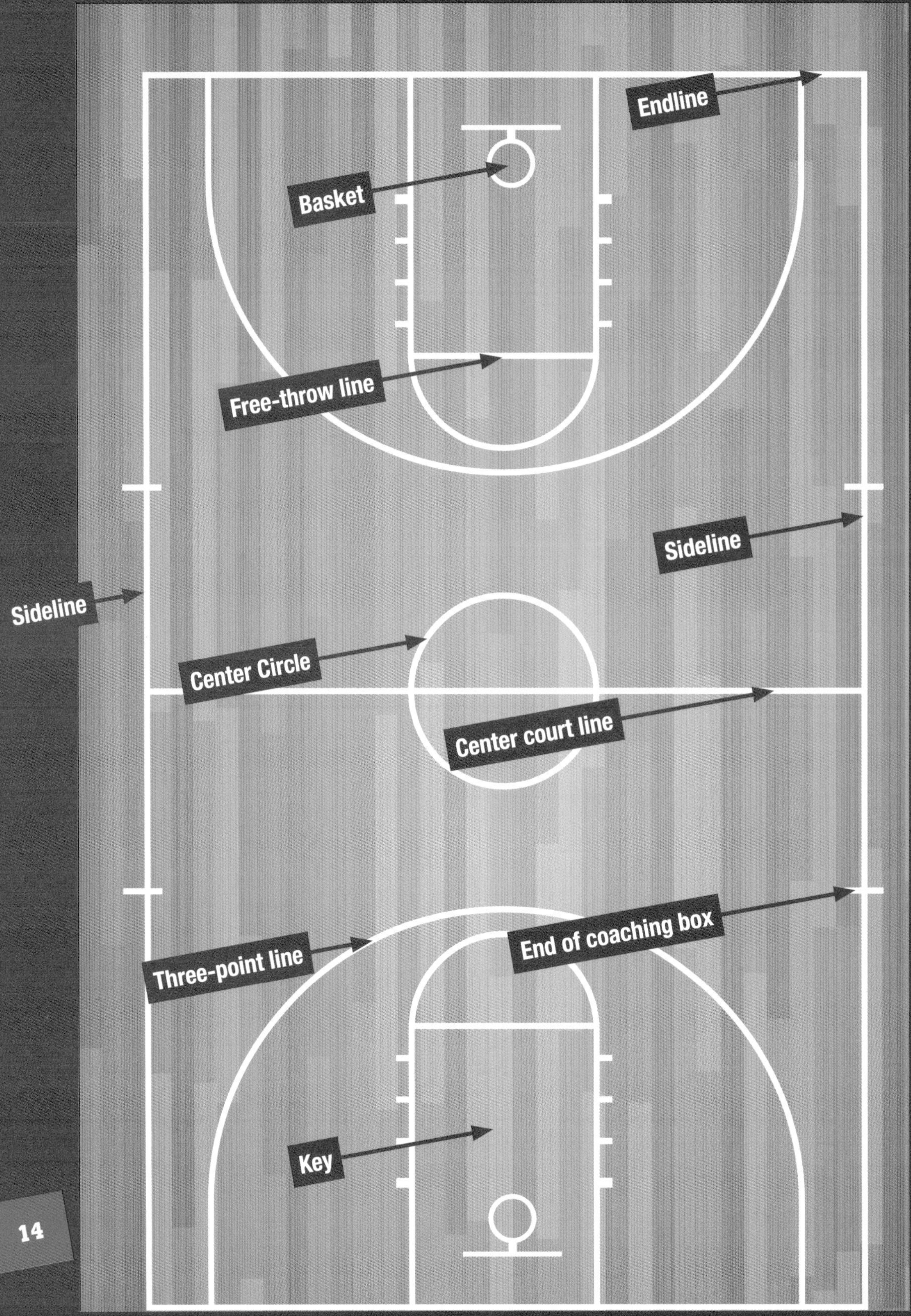

Endline

Basket

Free-throw line

Sideline

Sideline

Center Circle

Center court line

Three-point line

End of coaching box

Key

THE BASKETBALL COURT

An NBA court is 94 feet long and 50 feet wide (28.6 m by 15.24 m). Nearly all the courts are made from hard maple wood. Rubber mats under the wood help make the floor springy. Each team paints the court with its logo and colors. Lines on the court show the players where to take shots. The diagram on the left shows the important parts of the NBA court.

Oklahoma is home to many cowboys. So is the Thunder's home. The Chesapeake Energy Arena hosts several rodeos each year, including a pro bull riding event.

GOOD TIMES

When the team was in Seattle, it won the 1979 NBA championship. The SuperSonics beat the Washington Bullets to win the league title. Seattle also won the 1996 Western Conference title. Since moving to Oklahoma City, the team has not had a losing record for a season. The Thunder has won five Northwest Division championships.

17

Seattle Coach Lenny Wilkens was all smiles as he showed off the 1979 NBA championship trophy.

Jeff Green lost the ball on this play from 2008. The SuperSonics lost a lot of games that year, too!

TOUGH TIMES

The SuperSonics had a slow start in the NBA. In Seattle, they didn't make the playoffs for their first seven seasons. The team's final years in Seattle were not very good, either. They set a team record with 62 losses in 2007-08. The next year, the team moved. Things have really improved since the team became the Oklahoma City Thunder!

ALL THE RIGHT MOVES

Only a few NBA players earn a **triple-double**. That is a game in which a player averages double digits in three areas. For example, a player might have 22 points, 12 **assists**, and 10 **rebounds**. Oklahoma City **guard** Russell Westbrook is a triple-double master. In 2017, he had 42 triple-doubles. That is the most for a season in NBA history!

Russell Westbrook rises for a shot in 2017 over Cleveland's LeBron James. Westbrook can do it all on the court!

Gary Payton played 13 seasons of his Hall of Fame career with Seattle.

HEROES THEN

Spencer Haywood was one of the league's top scorers in his five Seattle seasons. Center Jack Sikma played nearly every game in his nine seasons with Seattle. He led the team to its only NBA title. Guard Gary Payton was the team's best player ever. He was a nine-time All-Star. Payton was named to the **Basketball Hall of Fame** in 2013. Kevin Durant led the NBA in scoring four times in nine seasons with the SuperSonics and Thunder.

HEROES NOW

All-around star Russell Westbrook leads the Thunder. He is good at every part of the game. He has led the NBA in scoring twice. Forward Paul George is also among the NBA's top players. He can score from just about anywhere on the court. Steven Adams grew up in New Zealand. At seven feet (2.13 m) tall, he helps get the ball to Westbrook and George.

Reaching up for a dunk is a piece of cake for seven-foot (2.13 m) center Steven Adams.

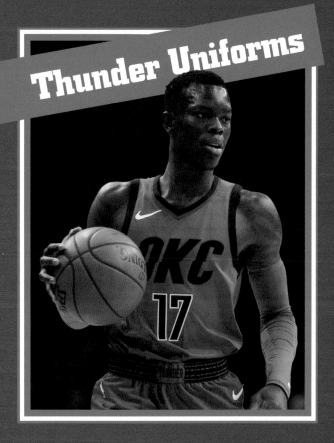

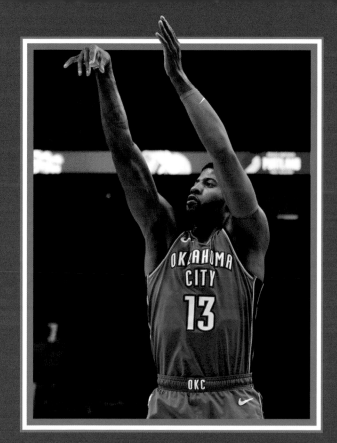

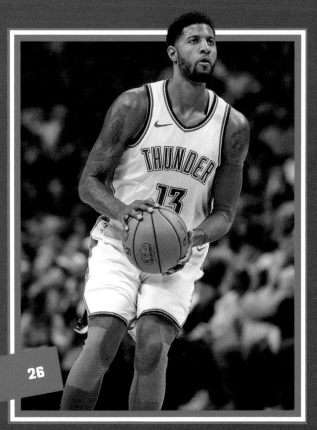

WHAT THEY WEAR

NBA players wear a **tank top** jersey. Players wear team shorts. Each player can choose his own sneakers. Some players also wear knee pads or wrist guards.

Each NBA team has more than one jersey style. The pictures at left show some of the Thunder's jerseys.

The NBA basketball (left) is 29.5 inches around. It is covered with leather. The leather has small bumps called pebbles.

The pebbles on a basketball help players grip it.

TEAM STATS

Here are some of the all-time career records for the Oklahoma City Thunder. These stats are complete through all of the 2018–19 NBA regular season.

GAMES

Gary Payton	999
Fred Brown	963

POINTS PER GAME

Kevin Durant	27.4
Paul George	25.0

ASSISTS PER GAME

Lenny Wilkens	9.0
Russell Westbrook	8.4

THREE-POINTERS

Kevin Durant	1,143
Rashard Lewis	973

STEALS PER GAME

Slick Watts	2.5
Gus Williams	2.3

FREE-THROW PCT.

Ricky Pierce	.906
Ray Allen	.899

REBOUNDS PER GAME

Spencer Haywood	12.1
Jack Sikma	10.8

JACK SIKMA

assists *(uh-SISTS)* passes that lead directly to a basket

Basketball Hall of Fame *(BASS-ket-ball HALL UV FAYM)* a building in Springfield, Massachusetts, that honors the game's best players, coaches, and others

guard *(GARD)* a player in basketball who usually dribbles and makes passes

hurricane *(HUR-uh-kayn)* a swirling, wind-driven storm that moves from the ocean to land

mascot *(MASS-kot)* a costumed character who helps fans cheer

rebounds *(REE-bowndz)* missed shots that bounce back to the players on the court

rivals *(RY-vuhlz)* two people or groups competing for the same thing

tank top *(TANK TOP)* a style of shirt that has straps over the shoulders and no sleeves

triple-double *(TRIP-ul DUB-ul)* the feat of averaging double-digits in three statistics in one game or in one season

FIND OUT MORE

IN THE LIBRARY

Goodman, Michael E. *NBA Champions: Oklahoma City Thunder.* Mankato, MN: Creative Paperbacks, 2018.

Kortemeier, Todd. *Russell Westbrook (Biggest Names in Sports).* New York, NY: Focus Readers, 2018.

Sports Illustrated Kids (editors). *Big Book of Who: Basketball.* New York, NY: Sports Illustrated Kids, 2015.

ON THE WEB

Visit our website for links about the Oklahoma City Thunder:
childsworld.com/links

Note to Parents, Teachers, and Librarians: We routinely verify our Web links to make sure they are safe and active sites. So encourage your readers to check them out!